kid.

a teeny book of POEMS

FOR KATHY
A fellow kid
AND playmate on
this playground
of life

♡ Christine ♡

dedication.

for my
mom ♡

who fixes my heart when it feels broken,
my head when it feels cloudy,
my hands when they feel tired, and
my self when it feels empty.

Oh!
AND A few
DRAwings.

kid.

a teeny book of
POEMS

be.

I'm lost and not here
But what if I could
Find the place where the
Line of the world stood

And the sand would do wonders
for my deep ocean blue
Complex with jade emeralds
Overwhelmed from the new

Tides could pull in fresh fear
But push cloudy pain out
Clean wounds with pink salts
Turn guilt into nothing foamy spouts

I'm in search and not found
But I'm on a shore
Near the place where the
Line of the world soars.

anticipation

Connection

of novelty

ok.

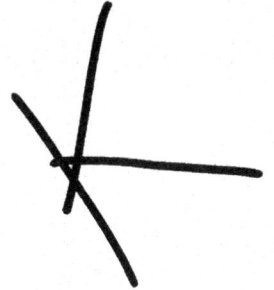

alright
      oh well
we'll see
            maybe
    so what
          no way
  here, stay
what
           hey
  for real
      you mean
   tonight
      like now
this thing
    gee whiz
             i know
you do
       for sure
   k, boo.

prowl

About last week
there was a moment
where leaves stood still

And the winds of time crunches
Stopped and looked to
the right

And all of the sky said Hi
Hey you
You're beautiful
And exactly where you should
Be

This fire is yours
Here
Forged by friendships
And eye contact

Rooted in the ground
You found
And walked down
Paths you chose and
Circles you decided on

A life unexplored leads
Well I don't know
I'm still hiking up
A rocky gorge I found
Gorgeous

prowl.

Levels and seasons
And many mystery drizzles
Of rain and sun and an autumn
All those reasons

Lessons

What am I saying
Well I don't know
I'm just typing on an iPhone
In meatpacking

The goddess of all words
(exper i ence)
She builds those
raw muscles
Sore from exploring
From a life, well, lived
At a picnic table
On a Sunday In Phoenicia

Let me get my hair dyed
While I drink my beat juice
And think about the tiny tide
Pulling my mind
down and up
Up and right

Smiling about it all
And prowling on a jagged line
Somewhere

Hey, whats over there...

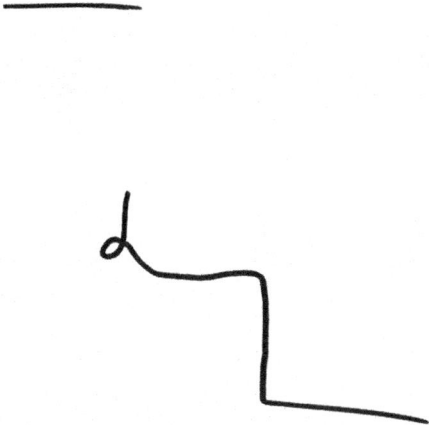

change.

just dropped on the ground
the floor caught it
but put it in its mouth
swallowed it whole
the quarter and all
i asked for my receipt
Change just stared at the wall.

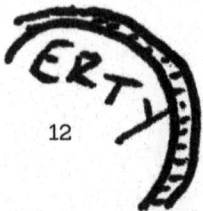

label.

christine

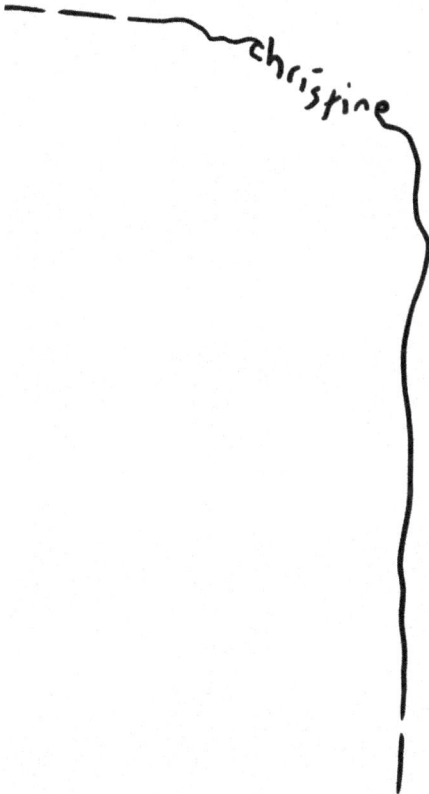

Rain in my name
streaks on the page
drips in the letters
drops on the shape
damp in the C
wet in the E
and the middle part
washed away down the street.

no water please, just ocean

island.

Wonder if waves feel crash on rocks

Wonder if rocks miss parts that fall off

Wonder if stars whisper nonono when fading out

Wonder if sun begs time to let it sleep in, just for right now

Wonder if moon grips hug from light spiraling around

Wonder if clouds know heartbreak while colors bleed down

Wonder if breeze loses speed if it forgets the point

Wonder why I can't seem to feel right if left to a straight

Should.

concrete

The bricks are slowly being laid
Don't worry
The concrete won't dry

For I'm learning every single day
The answers come
and fade away

Forever and ever we build and change
Making plans and shifting gaze

Thinking a thought that splits in two
Taking a big step then forgetting what to do

Spotting our star then losing our sight
Finding a direction then seeing red lights

Believing in something until the whole thing seems crazy
Stopping ourselves when we come to a maybe

It's swirling around a concrete plan
That's wet and soupy and will never end

Because we are driven by that never ending question
That attaches itself to everything like a punctuation

It sits in the middle of our spirit and smiles
For it's hungry and curious and never tires

concrete.

It keeps us going like a pulse we can't ignore
And beats for our soul, the reason for it all

It's the dance partner to a lonely mind
And the battle-axed knight defending age from time

It protects against the villains of prejudice
Forcing questions of clarity and moments of tenderness

It listens and learns and listens some more
(For it's a piece of you that is quite pure)

It simply won't die until you ignore it
Like all things precious, we must adore it

Which I would recommend to you, my friend
Snub this piece and your world will end

For nothing goes past a decided upon answer
If we don't follow our instincts and press further

With that single word that lives in our head
Repeating itself over and over again

Our curiously wishful dreamy lullaby
We hear you we hear you

Keep asking WHY.

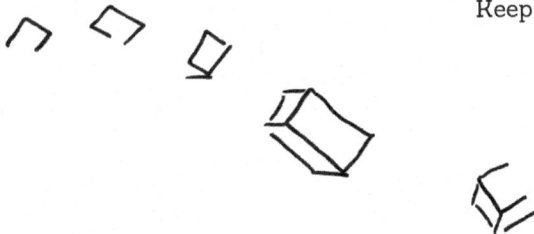

paint with fire

if the canvas burns,
well done.

angel town.

you're really
doing it for me
Currently
Kisses to you
And your edges
So swirly
Retro Divorced from
That old east coast
Purity
Ease and thrill and
Vegan entrees
Concurrently
With surf and neon
And a boulevard
for Barbie,
With fluff and grunge
and diaspora valet
you're an oasis where everyone
is their own well
and a desert for those
who don't mind sweat
oh baby or
or babe you prefer
I love you
angel town kisses to
all of your
subtle barbarity.   19

sparks

Isn't it nice

we know the sun will set
and we know the moon will rise

and we know the stars are out there
beyond the cloudy shade of midnight

and even though we can't tonight
see those stars that burn and churn
Oblivious to time,
chilling
behind that persistent city light
Tonight,

We can still look up
and smize, sigh and nod

at our friends, the stars

Those twinkly ambitions
And

Isn't it nice to know they are there

sparks.

Polka dots of glitter
Sparks who picked
Dare

Isn't it nice to know
Like the sun and the moon,
we can see them too

Not with our eyes but in our mind

an inside belief that goes
Endless and without sides
Isn't it nice to know

we can believe in our imagination
Tonight.

behind mirrors.

They have the darkest shades
Pains and aches
    that know no name
They point and laugh
    and disintegrate
On a stage with a mic
    for ears to salivate
The joy of their Them
    and the belly of our laugh
Is known from the source
    of the second half
The other side, the upside down
    Flip it over and turn it around
Hiding behind a love of mirrors
    Sits the tragedy of joke
    in a blazer of fear
To know the one,
    they must know the other
Face it and name it
    and brave the water
Isn't life perfect in its entirety
Comedians can live with both and do it
    Truthfully.

only new in a city once.

You know the year
    Flashing in my eyes
        stinging and pulsing
and
  suggesting a goodbye
     to tiny bits of color
I painted in the air
     living in a memory
   forever nowhere.

front doors

Once in a land
where

beginnings never end
where laughter carries cement
where cowards crack and bend

A step with a shadow
beckoned
It lunged and hit my
abdomen

It begged for an ascension

It pleaded and
prodded and
peppered with
persuasion
and
perpetually
paused to create
lasting tension

It aggregated and
agitated and
arguably annoyed the
arbitration
aroused by the announced
elevation

front doors.

And never oh ever
will I climb this said step
Forever means never
will I touch these laid bricks

As I stand far away in
the shadow of the sun
Gazing upon a setting day
bleeding alone

I notice the sounds and the air
and the taste
I thank mood for the glow
of my renegade days.

And walk away down a path
towards another frame

I smile, it's not bad, this
lonely wet heat

Front doors live
for your secrets to keep

For this is not mine,
this step over here
So I'll go home now thank you

I don't just climb anywhere.

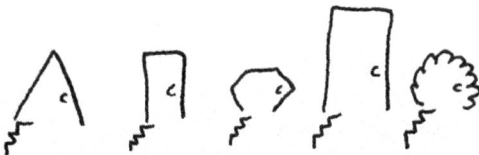

hold.

I'm a lava rock
  chipped
down so much I'm
  dripping
black sand
  Covered
head to toe
  with stuff from the
promises land
  Center of the earth
  in the middle of my mind
Hope the green roots
  Can
hold me before the
  high tide.

scribble.

this is a mistake
i didn't put it here
that ink on this page
that dash over there
just pretend i didn't
it's totally fine
that dash over there
has never been mine.

Time means Eternity
I think we made up seconds minutes hours to attempt
Sanity

heartiness.

I feel like my heart
Lives in my ribs
Caged by the trials
Of behind and late
Aging thoughts matching
Aging bones
My heartiness breaks behind
Its throne

Ribbed inside
caged by time.

place.

And the World went back to the way it was

And the Black fell back to the shade it knows

And the Cup was empty and the Heart was full

And the Air was hot and the Bed was cold

And everything stopped

And nothing happened

And Regret sank into the soft padded right hand

And the Whys took a seat on the floor by the door

And the Lonelys laid down because they couldn't anymore

And the Room was blank except for a chair

And that Chair held its ground in the sun over there

And the Sun widened its gaze to cover the space

And remind all the sad things they too have a place.

heir.

Mid
Drifting
through a
Chain fence
Neighbors play their
Music
Loud and trumpet filled
Roulette
On this backyard alley
Closet
Thinking my mind is a
Raisinet
Dried up fake sugar coated in
Chocolate
Forgive forgive me five year old
Cadet
Frozen hard eyes holding for the
Moment
When I feel the age creep into my
Crows nest
Welcome enemy of timing
you forgetful,
Lady Regret.

past and future are always with us in present
- they go by the name . instinct.

system.

this isn't polish

it's sweat

and tears and some of my

rain condensing in my

ears, screaming

listen

soul

you inner atmosphere

take it and make it

into

condensensation

clear?

or

at least

make water

so that my brain

in my heart in my lungs

can drink in that air

changed

from way deep down

in there.

He is Climate.
I am Weather.

greygray.

There's nothing wrong
it's just not right
there's nothing black
there's nothing white
there's nothing here
why would there be
because it's not you
and it isn't me
it's both of us
in a vacant space
with heavy air
and no chairs
we both want to move
but we can't find the edge
where the vacant ends
and the something begins.

final movie credit

Outside,
somewhere new.
Hard to see, but the sky was blue.

The sun was falling
The ground was sprawling
Every which way it wanted to.

And all the yesterdays
felt comfortable and inclined
Gently knocking on the door
of next week and beyond.

The past was present
meaning we knew where we left it
And our eyes were up
instead of reticent.

This was back a month or a few
November perhaps or an eon ago.

Before the slumber
of everyday normal
Became a numbing of questions
streaming live on insomnia.

Like a bone without marrow
A bow without an arrow

(I guess flares shoot off, live, then die alone somewhere in the air)

final movie credit.

BUT, WAIT, beginnings can only exist with an end?
Guess our world forgot basic story mechanics.

Still,

the big chunky boulder big luminous rocks
they sit on top of this shifting other rock
they live and they breath as they spin and spin
knowing the horizon line will eventually appear
again and again.

And, I guess, stories begin ...
again and again.
Ya...I'm ignorant to think endings even really exist.

If the horizon line is our final movie credit
then it's the opening line
of the other half's early morning edit

Huh.

I'm Outside,
somewhere new again.
Hard to see, but the sky is still blue-ish
The sun still comes up
And the ground still holds us down and

Every which way I think
a new thought is found.

Thanks for saying out loud the things i say
alone in my throat

rugged.

If the weathered skin of memories in my head

Could soften and lean into a comfortable position

Rest their weary head on my mind and not think about time

Breath in long and deep without worry or deceit

Shrug their shoulders

Turn up their mouth corners

And lock eyes with our friend the present moment

Our rugged memories of a lifetime past

Could tell us our stories

To help us relax.

poet.

used to write poems

Driving backward towards the sermons

Thinking forward for the stop signs

Looking up and seeing airplanes

I used to write poems

Nudging moods to the alleyways

Skipping waze and going 1950s

I used to write poems

In the Forever or never

my life confined to a

Forgotten moment parked

On a corner in the sun by

A broken lamp pole palm tree

I used to write.

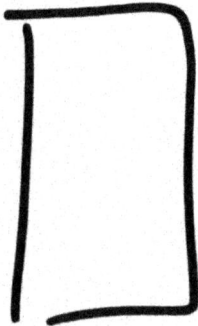

home.

In the dark of the night

with the Stars out there
somewhere

Despair, sits cold and steaming
defiantly knowing that the stars

well
they don't shine for Her

and this Despair
sighs and laments
cries and convinces

She curls up and screams out:
STARS
YOU STARS SOMEWHERE
WHY AM I NOT GOOD ENOUGH
WHY DON'T YOU CARE

the Stars whisper back:
We care, Despair
We shine and shine
searching for You
but You're hiding somewhere

come out of there, Despair
come out to Our somewhere.

the no in no one is the only no i know.

announcement.

Bruised and single and deeply engaged

Deeply involved and, yes, deeply engaged

Engaged in my hands and the things that they make

Engaged in my feet and the hips that they sway

Engaged in my eyes and the photos they take

Engaged in my buds and those yummy flavors they taste

Engaged in my brain, I mean it's writing this thing

Engaged in it all and to?

Engaged to my soul

for bruises or worse, engaged to the whole.

floating.

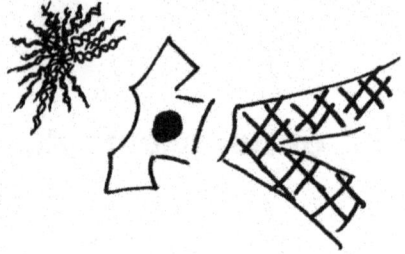

Linoleum floor on a Friday
Feels nice on my skin
Cool bae
Wild in an empty kitchen
Caught hungry, wait, haunted
Wanted
Needed
Nah empty
Limited to the hour
And the size of my shower
The less of me equals
A blank floor
With no sequins
Stop shock and
Kiss the floor before
My gravity evaporates
Heartless means hopeless
Stop being depressing
But
How do I sleep when I'm
Floating on the ceiling?

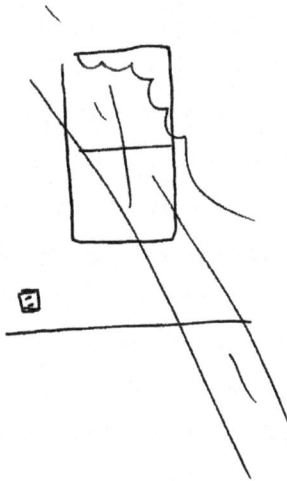

vision through panels
horizon divided into frames

points with a view
not blind in my room

ink.

the life lived

is stained on a page

smudged in the lines

smushed there beside

words we remember

and periods we forget

commas we added

and nouns we made subjects

writing it down is like

running out of ink

there's more I can add

but my brain pen

can't

Think

shhhhhhh.

Don't wanna talk
Nothing to say
Don't need a pep talk
It's a different kind of day
Don't want the lights on
But that firelight's ok
Don't feel like smiling
Not right now, anyway
Don't need a hug
But I'd like you to stay
Don't wanna talk
Nothing...

Well, everything to say

Don't know where to start
I know, there's no right way.

losing guard

Nightime
　　　in a red dress
i feel it in my toes
　　　and in my head
piano is on the TV
and the memory
　　　of the love i had for you and me
me and me
green light
humming
　　　birds in the dark can't be seen
　　　just heard chirping
i feel the dinner i made in my hands
pasta caked into my nail beds
bed covered in clothes i didn't wear
　　　and shoes on my feet,
　　　updo in my hair
i'm serious
about the things i'm crazy about
　　　excited is a word i overuse
　　　other people say weird
sure use defenses
label a space with a door
pour more or take it slow
　　　ducky was pretty
　　　arthur had a sword
i want a kid
i am

but i want a reason for
well, to(o)

losing guard.

what happens when the rest of your life

is seen
and you know, ya know, you know
        i'm sweating
and nodding
and feel happy
        in the tips of my eye lashes
like they might drip
drop with the rush of the maybe
        the next maybe
        is the last
        maybe
never is a horrible word
so is love
        both so finite.
did i mention
i'm serious
about the never
being a never?
        listen
        i hear you
nighttime in a red dress
with
hands pumping
        blood down to click
breath pounds out because
        well it's more escaping out
        i'm sick
because well, i'm a losing guard
        never is a terrible word
        but it has the word ever in it too
ever never forever.
bring it.

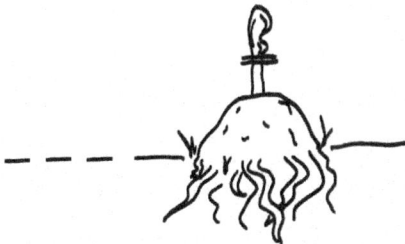

49

life on the fly
small falls with the highs
sunlight opening squinty eyes
perfection in disguise

long weekend.

I'm not at a beach or a bbq
not with a boy or with a big group
not on a hike or a waterfall
not running late or
wishing someone would call
not sad or mad or agitated
not lonely or grumbly or
FOMO sedated
I'm not doing anything
Anything at all
just sitting on the floor
alone,
breathing good and long
I'm leaning near my door
thinking about the Fall
Not bad, this holiday
Not bad at all.

for a friend.

Balance takes practice
And
Plants take nutrients
And
Hearts take healing
And
Breath takes feeling
And
Love takes patience
And
Life takes focus
And
Everything in between
takes a moment of silence.

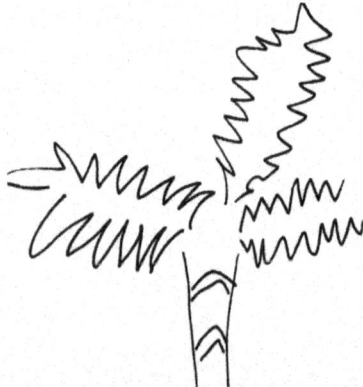

holy.

Hollywood, my pet
    That's what it's called
Hollywood, my dove
    It's quite unequalled
Hollywood, my sweet
    Nope, no bushes or trees
Hollywood, my love
    It grows from dreams.

so on it

Love my surprise balloon, reaching for the stars
  (cute little bubble of a pink kiss heart)

Love that I'm allowed to wear whatever I want
  (body is planted in twink soil style art)

Love the life I've lived and where I currently am
  (koreatown lounging in sequins doing Puppy car writing)

Love the present feeling, love the present me
  (what a present we all are, on this Valentine's Day)

Love not knowing why we all started existing
  (happy to be a part of our species of human being)

Love the mystery of self and all the deep excavating
  (that final frontier of soul sure has endless storyline possibilities)

Love the boundless questions, love the spontaneous epiphanies
  (love love love that I'm also allowed to dislike things)

so on it.

Love you and us and this world, even when it's tough
　　(because we can heal, I'm sure, if we don't give up)

And we will win if we love our insides most of all
　　(since the best love comes out when we practice on our own soul)

So I'll keep falling back in love with past and future me
　　(and give that same love out to every person I see)

I'll keep opening my mind as I open my heart
　　(for friendships are built on an open floor plan with an honest start)

And the more I wonder about what love really means
the more this surprise little balloon bounces up to say Hi
　　(from my car seat)

Reminding me that our pal Love is ready to be felt all the time,
it's next to us, inside of us, it is yours and it is mine

We're allowed to feel it everyday, for everything
　　(isn't that nice?)

It's two o'clock on a Friday
and I bumped into a balloon

It reminded me love feels like freedom
and then followed me home.

we are always in-between something.

we are in-between past and future, birth and dying, the end of a
moment and the beginning of the next.

what even is 'being present' when we exist in constant change?
there is space between our fingerprints for a reason, we couldn't see
each line if there weren't a space.

solace is seeing the end of something and the beginning of the next
thing, maybe the current numbing is the end of something?

or...just the beginning.

lullaby.

Sleep now, my Bunny

Before the stars set
Before the yellow glows
Before the night goes

Sleep now, my Bunny

Before the dreams escape
Before the breath elevates
Before the embers of your eyes
Cascade
up and out and beyond

Sleep now, my Bunny

Tomorrow's horizon with be drawn
And dried and ready
For you to then play on

Sleep now, my Bunny
Dream on.

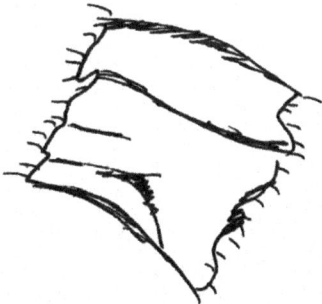

a woman stands

A woman stands with open arms
Not in spite, just because
There is purpose in Constance
For these arms she holds her whole life for me

A woman stands with open eyes
Clear and full of salt and sweat
She never blinks or lowers shade
For these eyes gaze upon the life I lead

A woman stands with open heart
Raw and exposed pointed straight at me
With her arms wide and her eyes pointed soft
At a heart she started with the first beat

A woman stands
She does not sit
She does not shift or move away
She stands beside or behind or in front
And stands wherever I need her to be

a woman stands.

This woman made me
This woman knows me
This woman remembers and never forgets me

This woman Stands and holds and sees me
With forever an open heart that watches and
Beats to protect me

Never can I give what she has given
The weight and breath she held has been lived in

All I can do is continue to tell her
How to hold me
How I see me
How to love me

This woman stands for all of me to be Free.

smile.

I found a smile inside
my phone
I don't know where it's from
I'll dedicate it to...
to the day as a whole
Yes, you Day, to all of you
you did a good job
I'll thank your sun for
coming out to play
And thank your stars for
peeking out again
I'll wish that our friends
feel good and whole
And hope,
in sleep, they dream
and they soar
I'll close my eyes and breath in time
And smile again, in my real life
Then share this little moment
with you because
this little lost smile needs something to do
I'll save it here
so Tomorrow can see
All the joy that
your Today gave me.

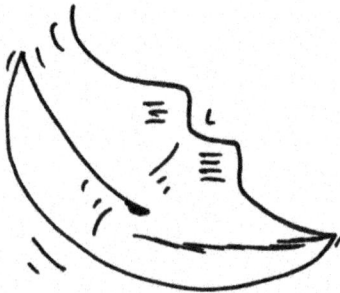

re:

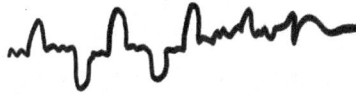

You're my forever savior and king and leader and captain
You're my forever friend and confidant and soulmate and secret weapon

You're my forever shoulder and bear hug and slap in the face
Forever phone call and dry matchbox and umbrella when it rains

If I'm scared of the dark, you'll find me a nightlight
if I want to see the stars, you'll build me a skylight

Never ever for the rest of my life can I say
how much you have given me or
how much of me you have saved

Never ever for the rest of my life will I stop
striving to give all of it back to you
however I can
past forever and beyond.

rambling behind lights invisible

and
growing brighter by imagination

forever.

belongs to each person

individually

differently

defined by me

For my forever

   is only mine, forever

because

it begins

continues

And ends with me.

free clouds

I collected all the clouds
My clouds
And put them in a bottle

Well, an old mason jar
Cleaned and honest
Smelling of jelly, tart cherry
Ready for the cloud clotting

The clouds were plump
And happy for a trip
I snatched 'em up and pushed 'em in

They looked around
Their fresh cherry house
Floated up and floated down
Clotted and spread
And collected again
As if they wanted me to think
They were considering

But every time I reached for my lid
They stared up at me and
Evaporated

These tricky clouds
My blustery boisterous mounds
They just weren't listening

free clouds

I stared at them as they stared at me
With hope in their cloud shadows
What were my dreams thinking?

I shined down with a reassuring smile
"Come, clouds, take a break, escape the wind,
Be your true self for awhile

Find your shape and settle down,
With a cloth roof and clear walls
You can finally be unwound

You'll be safe and you'll be sound
To float up and float down
With a solid base to keep you on the ground
Don't you see, it's like you're free!
Just how dreams are supposed to be"

My clouds stopped mid air
And rushed towards me
Smelling of cherry as I intended them to be
Shaped like a jar as I suggested them to be

They lingered low and thin
Hardly existing
Not how I imagined my dreamy clouds living

free clouds

They sighed:
Do you see us now, dear friend,
After all your insisting?
Do you see how we become
When YOU are not listening?

Your plan to protect simply makes us die
We can't settle or relax or escape the sky

What would dreams be if they couldn't evaporate
And blow and break and form and condensate

We have to die to be able to live
Since freedom is formed from a place of risk

So, keep your jar, dear friend
And your cherry smell too
We love you for protecting us
Really we do
But we got to be dreams
We've got to, for you.

And this, this made me lean in
Very close to my clouds
My floating dreams that are made
From deep down inside my insides

I leaned in as they whispered
So fluffy soft and light
I leaned in as they whispered
You know you're the wind, right?

free clouds.

You make us and break us and make us again
We form from the visions clotted in your head

We open your jar locked up in your mind
And become what you see, there behind your eyes

We don't mind a breeze or a hurricane wind
We can handle breaking and forming again

You can't lose us. You just can't.
So stop saying you will.

I nodded, they're right, dreams live forever, ya know

I put away the jar and took a look in my mind
It was blowing a wind of a familiar size

My clouds gathered and moved, together again
Preparing to depart
On a new journey with an old wind

But before they went, they looked up at me
With hope in their cloud wrinkles, spurring,

Remove your lid, dear friend. Be free.

together.

Woah
I guess it's supposed to be
You are you
I am me
Them or us
That's where it starts
When we separate
And stand apart
So here's this thing
The in-between
The middle ground
The something missing
Our photo's still developing
We'll clear the blur
And find the frame
And feel complete
Together, in the end,
I've got your back
and you can just be
You beside me beside you
In our box of We.

70

index.
(pages)

{creation relic}

April 23 2020
I saw Monks Battle!
It can all Happen with
                    Presence!
AND I see You!!i
   i see you.

TallyHoe
Daily
Doodle +
Musing

During
Quarantine.

23

ackn oledg ments.

black pens
white paper
feelings
memory
parent's guest room
epistemology
the call to adventure.

kid.

Thank you for sharing in this experience with me.

Life is one big experiment, a map of hidden playgrounds. And I feel most alive making these experiences full of imagination.

Happy we could play on this playground together.

I share prose, poetry, plays, films, characters, and tales with all age groups and within a mixture of stages to build honest human connection.

Hope to see you again on another playground.

Christine HAUER xo

Made in USA - North Chelmsford, MA
1176962_9781734146806
12.20.2022 1504